what to say and do
to comfort
a bereaved mother

SOFTENING
THE GRIEF

JOAN E. MARKWELL
with
JANIE FIELDS
PATRICIA HOLLINGSWORTH
SUZIE McDONALD

DUDLEY COURT PRESS
SONOITA, AZ

Dudley Court Press
PO Box 102
Sonoita, AZ 85637
www.DudleyCourtPress.com

Cover and interior design by Dunn+Associates, www.Dunn-Design.com
Author photos by Digital Alliance

Markwell, Joan E., 1951- | Fields, Janie, 1954- |
Hollingsworth, Patricia (Patricia Ralston), 1954- | McDonald, Suzie (Suzie Vickers), 1955-
Softening the grief : what to say and do to comfort a bereaved mother /
Joan E. Markwell with Janie Fields, Patricia Hollingsworth, Suzie McDonald.
1st ed.
p cm.
Sonoita, AZ : Dudley Court Press, [2017]
ISBN: 978-1-940013-41-1 (paperback) | 978-1-940013-42-8 (mobi) |
978-1-940013-43-5 (epub) | LCCN: 2017942227

Children--Death. | Children--Death--Psychological aspects. | Mother and child. |
Mothers--Psychology. | Parental grief. | Bereavement. | Grief. | Death--Psychological aspects. |
Loss (Psychology) | Consolation. | BISAC: SELF-HELP / Death, Grief, Bereavement. |
PSYCHOLOGY / Grief & Loss.
LCC: BF575.G7 M37 2017 | DDC: 155.9/37092--

ISBN (paperback): 978-1-940013-41-1
ISBN (mobi): 978-1-940013-42-8
ISBN (epub): 978-1-940013-43-5
LCCN: 2017942227

To the children who have gone before us

Melissa Dawn Fields

Jamie Flynt

Keeley Knuteson Hollingsworth

Cynthia J. Peterson

Acknowledgments

We want to acknowledge all of the bereaved mothers who have contributed to this book. To those who have answered our questions, we thank you for your time and honesty. To those who could not answer our questions, we realize that says a lot also. Thank you.

We would also like to acknowledge:
Gay Barnard and Lisa J. Fields – Thank you for letting us bounce ideas off you.

Lisa G. Fields, Debbie Moore, and Cheryl Powell – Thank you for typing and listening.

Cheryl Steenerson – Thank you for adding all the commas and comments.

Kathy Buckman – Thank you for spending all of those hours typing and retyping and retyping.

Vicki Hicks - Thank you for digging through photographs.

John Greenwell and Suzan Johnson – Thank you for reviewing our manuscript and providing suggestions.

Barbara McNichol – Thank you for being the editor who saw the possibilities of using our experiences to help others.

Gail Woodard with Dudley Court Press – Thanks for taking us up a few (lots of) notches.

Kenneth Stevenson and Andrew Bennett with Digital Alliance – Thank you for the videos and photos.

Missy, Jamie, Keeley, and Cindy – Thank you for the legacy you have left behind. In turn, it allows your mothers to leave their legacies behind through this book, *Softening the Grief*.

Meeting Our Children

Through the pages of this book, we want you to know our four loved ones who left this earth too soon. By way of introduction, please read the brief descriptions of their lives and accomplishments in *Part V: Grateful Acknowledgments*.

Janie's daughter Melissa (Missy)

Suzie's son Jamie

Patty's daughter Keeley

Joan's daughter Cindy

Our Lifelong Secret

We belong to a secret society. Membership is mandatory to those who have lost a child. Without choice, they become lifetime members, keeping this secret close to their hearts until their final days.

We "members" stand by ourselves in a room full of people, but we're never alone. We carry this secret of painful loss everywhere. Holding it in can make us react in ways we can't predict, much less understand. We do our daily chores clutching this silent secret that engulfs our hearts, minds, and souls. Often, it sits heavy on shoulders already burdened with sadness.

We crave to know our loved ones aren't forgotten, yet we hide this secret inside because others run from its mention. Still, the sweet-sounding names of our beloved children remain our steadfast companions. And turning inward to hear their names again brings a spark of love that only we feel.

Joan Markwell
April 2017

Contents

Schooling from our hearts

"Breathe in. Breathe out. Breathe in. Breathe out.
Breathing in, then breathing out; that will make it go
away. Concentrate on that one thing, just breathing."

Yet try as we might, it keeps coming back. Our children's pain, their passings, and the unimaginable circumstances of their deaths will not leave our minds. There's no way of trying *not* to think that keeps the pain from enveloping our minds. It's simply not that easy.

Thus, we offer our help to assist bereaved mothers through a period that involves her worst nightmare—losing her child. Who knows the right thing to say or do for grieving mothers and those helping them cope with their loss?

"I can't believe you just said that to me." That phrase reflects the thoughts we often experience. Others' *unintentionally painful comments and actions* can make our grief journey all that more difficult.

A fresh understanding of this unimaginable loss prompted me to do *something* to ease the suffering of other grieving mothers. This is true for three other bereaved mothers who can provide insight into our minds as well as tools to assist other mothers needing comfort. *Softening the Grief* is the result.

We wrote this book to educate those who can make a difference in how bereaved mothers can be comforted, supported, and encouraged. Consider the advice within these pages a new way to console your grieving loved ones.

Our suggestions to you come from the heart. We don't condemn those who make thoughtless comments, nor are we angry with them.

We acknowledge that, until one experiences the life-changing trauma of losing a child, we are all pitifully uneducated to deal with grief of this magnitude.

Janie, Suzie, Patty, and Joan E.—all mothers of deceased children—have written this book from a grieving mother's viewpoint, not only ours but dozens of grieving mothers we've talked with. What's expressed in these chapters is felt by the majority of them. *Softening the Grief* doesn't pertain to a single event or something one person has said. Rather, these universal topics weave a common thread through the grief felt and shared by many we know and millions we don't know.

JOAN E. *I am a mother who has lost her child. I cannot process this alone. I need you. I know you can be there for me, if only you knew how. Let me show you the way. I have experienced the terror and trauma experienced by those who have somehow survived our children. Writing this book allows me to share hard-earned knowledge that can help you gain a better understanding of any bereaved mothers in your life. It can also help other grieving mothers by assuring them they aren't alone in their struggle to survive.*

Walking the grieving path can be less painful to both parties using the advice and stories shared in this book. We hope you walk away with a totally different viewpoint as you arm yourself with the information to make this possible.

Most of all, be present to love your children no matter what—for they aren't ours; God only loans them to us.

Why a Mother's Viewpoint

By writing this from a mother's viewpoint, we don't want to take anything away from others who are grieving. Fathers, spouses, children, grandparents, siblings, cousins, and a whole world of people have experienced the pain of losing a loved one. We choose to address a mother's pain only. Through the loss of

Missy, Jamie, Keeley, and Cindy, we feel qualified to offer tools as well as insight for surviving the stress and grief of losing a child or helping others who have. In particular, we address in Part II common painful phrases and situations that can help you know how to soften the grief they feel.

Living and Empathizing

We four authors are not psychologists or formally educated bereavement counselors. But we are highly qualified to discuss the pain a mother endures after losing her child as we are living through this grief journey and empathizing with others living it, too. We understand that happiness may take time to return to our lives and that patience and tolerance is necessary.

The situation is made even more painful by those who don't know what to say or do. They ignore us, say nothing, or make well-intentioned but thoughtless comments that can force us into further isolation.

Knowing we are inconsolable, it may seem best to give us space. In the beginning some may be constantly running and kicking away all human contact. Then we become aware that this deep, deep pain may never dissipate, and yet we have our lives to live.

During this time, we realize we are no longer rational people as we seemingly lose our sanity and struggle to fight our way back. We become isolated. Or is it that others have isolated themselves from us? Deep down, we're screaming for help. So help us—in the right way. Don't leave us because you think we're pulling you down with us. Instead, learn from us.

Where Do We Turn?

As we come out of the dazed world we're forced to live in, where do we turn? Commonly, best friends have dissolved away; husbands have witnessed our grief and cannot bear to hear more. We look down as we walk so we don't meet other people's eyes. We look down also so we don't have to see people enjoying their happiness. And we walk away from what's familiar, knowing our cherished children will never again enjoy the simple routines of this life. Rationalizing, we ask, "Why look up?"

Looking Up

Yet slowly, we look toward the sky seeking answers, help, hope, and compassion. There is no telling the damage we've done to the relationships we've neglected. We feel our regrets, and then we regret our regrets. The hurt and confusion leave us pacing and crying, then pacing and crying even more. Too much to remember. Not enough to remember. With so much confusion, we feel ourselves going crazy. Then we finally admit, "Oh yeah, I am crazy."

Chances are to others, we appear uncontrollable in our emotions and actions. That's why they try to control us. But how can anyone control the uncontrollable? You can't.

The Wavy Men

Mothers who have outlived their children become inflatable air dancers—you know, those wavy men blowing in the breeze? All of what made us who we were has been sucked out of us, leaving us with bodies blowing in the breeze. We exist and move forward without thought, even when we don't want to.

That's because our minds and bodies are no longer ours to control. Our physical bodies suffer from constant grief and stress. Our brains only think of unimaginable pain. There's little left that wants to push forward.

To those who love us, we need you to rein us in with subtle pushes. Point the way. Help hold us up. For it takes a long time before our bodies and minds return to a more familiar state. You don't realize the depth of our gratitude for your help that can give us the stability we need. Then we can once again allow our legs to hold us up and walk us in a positive direction—looking up.

Reading about our experiences in *Softening the Grief* gives you better understanding why we become the shells we once were— and how having a pair of crutches from you can support us.

Let us show *you* the way so you can show us the way.

Split Personality

We are so hurt, so mad, so stressed that often while going through this trauma, a split personality evolves: the old *me*, the new *me*, and the *me* yet to be. We feel neglected and abandoned, yet we miss being among people.

Over time, though, we are forgotten. We feel miserable long after the funerals, and friends tire of our grieving sighs. To the people closest to us—those who should be our allies—we become a burden, a threat, or an embarrassment.

We miss our old relationships terribly. We may or may not have the support of our spouse who's grieving, too, and can't offer much. Indeed, studies in the U.S. indicate the divorce rate of couples who have lost a child is as high as 25 percent. Living in the same household and expecting empathetic support from a spouse is frustrating for all. After all, men are designed to "fix" things. But this isn't "fixable."

Who Understands Us?

For most, all of our lives have been spent taking care of those close to us. When we ourselves are desperate for help, those we thought would care for us have scattered. So we make new friends; they understand us, tolerate us, and help us. Some of these new friends have also lost children, so we know how their pain feels. We don't have to *imagine* their pain; we *know* it firsthand.

We've gained a fresh understanding of those who suffer depression, anxiety, or any other mental disorder. After all, 228,000 children and young adults die every year in the U.S., so statistics tell us we're not alone. Plus we can now appreciate the lack of mental control a grieving state can cause. Being overcome by demons and emotions no longer allows us to be normal. Measured responses are no longer ours to make.

Forever Changed

The confident, strong person of old has suddenly become a weak, insecure, emotional wreck. Sometimes we step outside of our own bodies and look back, wondering what became of that "real" person we once were. The short-term effect has turned into a long-term lifestyle, or so it seems. For we are forever changed.

JOAN E. *I don't know who or what I will end up being. I just know I no longer am who I used to be.*

Still, everyone expects us to act like the person we once were. There are some days when, after finally getting a grip, we see the remnants of that old self—only to have the stool kicked out from under us time and again. It can be just a small thing—a minor disagreement, a particular friend, a certain song or screech of a siren on the road. Sometimes it's monumental—special weddings, holiday gatherings, our children not there when we're sick, and people who are around not understanding our feelings of frustration.

Out of Balance

Sadly, it's not only in our minds; it is physical, too. Our equilibrium seems out of balance. We experience an awkwardness we've never felt. Our hearts hurt in our chests. We have health issues. Our hair falls out and our hands shake. Sores invade, blood pressure soars, and illnesses appear.

At times, we can't mobilize or function. Our legs move woodenly. The weight on our hearts holds our whole body to the floor. Grief is so physically painful, we understand how people can commit suicide, rely on alcohol or pills, turn on their spouses, and even die from it.

Pain Never Recedes

Ever received such bad news about a loved one's accident or dire diagnosis that leaves a knot in your stomach akin to being punched? Ever had a sudden ache in your heart for that person? Imagine how it feels to live with that pain that never recedes.

Our children's deaths are stuck in *our* minds, not *their* lives. The suffering and the circumstances stay with us. It is hard to get past the dying part and on to examining the lives they lived. Our language identifies widows, widowers, and orphans. But for a Mother who loses a child, we remain nameless. No word identifies us succinctly.

Consequently, we blame ourselves, we blame others, we blame doctors, and we blame God. We seem mad at everything and everyone. Mostly, we are angry with ourselves. For as the mothers, we are the protectors of our young.

Crazy Link Among Bereaved Mothers

There has to be a common, crazy link among bereaved mothers. Even though each mourns in her own way, the crazy link prevails. And when one finds a group of crazies like herself, it feels like a crazy relief.

And that crazy grief changes over the years. The veteran griever in our group of four has eleven years under her belt, while our newest griever is eighteen months into it. No matter the lifestyle, skin color, nationality, or age of the children, we mothers are constantly climbing our way out of our grief. And some can climb better than others.

To Our Loved Ones and Friends

We know you love us and want to help us. Therefore, the four of us willingly go down this road together to open eyes. After hearing about a scenario and that person adds, "I felt that way, too," we know we are on the right track.

Although we cannot cover every situation, we hope that among the list of phrases and explanations in this book, you're better able to deal with the grieving process of those who are so unfortunate to belong to this unwanted society.

One Final Note

We love our families and friends. Maybe that's why their words hurt us the most. We only wish they could give us a "pass" for a couple of years, at least. Allow us to scream, make stupid decisions, or say the wrong things without any repercussions. *Just let us be.* Let us make our mistakes and behave poorly.

We desperately need to "float" for a time; we can't handle life normally. Our feelings and emotions are so raw, we wear them on the outside of our skin instead of the inside. Lordy, we hurt so much.

We need our families and friends. We have missed you. And we ask you to gradually welcome us back with open and forgiving arms. As you do, please accept that the advice we offer here comes from our hearts and souls.

PART I

WHAT IT FEELS LIKE

TO LOSE A CHILD

I am hollow but you can help fill me.

I'm gasping for breath but you can help me breathe slowly.

I continue to shed tears, and you can cry with me.

I am lost in this crowd, but you can find me.

I am anxious and afraid, so I need you to protect me.

I feel so alone; I need you to be with me.

I am misunderstood; I need you to understand.

I no longer fit in; I need you to help me find my new me.

My heart is broken. I need your love.

— JOAN E.

CHAPTER 1

What a bereaved mother is feeling . . .

. . . The First Week

. . . The First Month

. . . The First Year

. . . Years to Follow

. . . Birthdays, Holidays, and Anniversaries

. . . Day of Death Anniversary

Two Years Later

Thought by now I'd find some peace

But the turmoil never seems to cease

Love, laughter, and life almost there

Then the heart develops another tear

Keep looking up for some of your strength

Simply can't reach too far its length

Left behind seems forever to doom

My heart buried as in a tomb

Waiting for the day to gaze upon you

Releasing my love again to arise anew

—JOAN E.

Typically, here's what bereaved mothers experience as time marches on

The First Week

We wake up with a heavy heart every morning. While pulling around a ball and chain, we're expected to take care of everyday business like it's a normal day.

However, we can get stuck in the "first day" of the "last day"— one that's remembered so clearly. The rest of the week with visitation, funeral services, receptions, and more blurs by comparison. We can't remember who came to the visitation and don't have a clue who was at the funeral. Now we know. (That's what guest registers are for!)

The First Month

Can't live without our loved one.
We're still sorting out what to do with new routines, jobs, and "normal" activities that aren't normal any more.

The First Six Months

The worst time of all.

The grief dictates our lives. Realizing we're losing control. Not seeing an end to the pain literally (and we mean "literally") drives us crazy. As the body reacts to the stress we feel, physical pain follows. Sleep is out of the question!

Seeing how others react to our loved one's death is confusing. We become hermits—not answering the phone, not going to church or the mall or even the grocery store for fear of seeing someone we know. It's not that we don't want to see them; we just can't face anyone without tearing up.

The first time we meet a friend since the death occurred can be frightening. We're tormented by the idea that our family is no longer "our family" and we're overwhelmed with fear that something bad could happen to our remaining loved ones.

The First Year

More of the first six months but different.

We live in fear of never feeling better. We question if we'll ever socialize again. A state of denial still surrounds us. We are riding a roller coaster. A downward run can set us back. We experience such thoughts as "You were good yesterday, so what's the matter with you today?" We realize we're on a lifetime journey with lapses into a dark hole.

JOAN E *Three hundred sixty-five days . . . not long enough. Move on—never. Get over it. How can I? I'll always be looking back. Cindy as my baby. Cindy as a young girl. Cindy as a sister. Cindy as a beautiful young lady. Cindy as a wife. Cindy as a mother. Cindy, my best friend. Every aspect of our lives was entwined together. I cherish the legacy she leaves behind in endless moments each day.*

Years to Follow

Even after two years, the experience is still very raw.

JOAN E *Not long ago someone said to me, "But that was two years ago!" Yes, it may have been two years, but it was like yesterday for me. The death, the circumstances, and others' reactions are still a tapestry of painful memories.*

Recently I met a 92-year-old aunt I never knew existed. She told me she had lost a child, tearing up as she said this. I knew that painful feeling instantly, too, as I know I will when I'm 92 years old.

Commemorating Birthdays, Holidays, and Anniversaries

"Were you sad all day?" Someone asked a mother this question the day of her child's birthday. Really!

Birthdays for bereaved mothers differ greatly from death anniversaries. We rejoice in the births of our children. Though it's a bittersweet joy, it allows us time to acknowledge our luck in having had them in our lives. We look back on their lives and all the memories we shared. We laugh, tell stories, and avoid thinking about losing them. Instead, we make plans to celebrate their lives and honor their memories. For example, when one bereaved mother received a cake for her child's birthday, it brought her joy thinking of the giver's thoughtfulness.

SUZIE *I celebrated my son Jamie's birthday 25 days after losing him. I released 34 balloons on his first birthday at the cemetery. Remembering my son on his birthday is extremely difficult. However, I spend the day with him, sometimes taking birthday cake, plates, forks, and napkins. I set the table so visiting family and friends can share in on his birthday. Those who come by tell stories about him. He was such a joker and always loved a good laugh.*

PATTY *Oh my, how Keeley loved to celebrate her birthday! To this day we celebrate it in a big way with her favorite steak dinner plus cake and ice cream. We rejoice in the fact that she's remembered and has enriched our lives. Sad, indeed, but always celebrated!*

JANIE *Having a birthday party for someone not on this earth is difficult. Our family has tried many ways to celebrate Missy's birthday. Thus far, nothing has given the peace we seek. Maybe someday.*

I want her birthday to be a day of joy just as it was when I gave birth to her. Usually, nobody says her name during the celebration, talking all the way around Missy and the wonderful heart prints she left. This hurts on that day especially.

On her birthday, I relive so many memories—the many firsts and accomplishments in her life, her friends, her laughter, and her beautiful smile. We recall her love of dancing, of her Dalmatian, Skyler, and of her many cats. I'm so blessed to have had my precious Missy."

Day of Death Anniversary

JOAN E *As I write this, I am one week from my daughter being gone two years. Like a cat on a hot tin roof, I feel edgy, nervous, just thinking about it. Seven days to go. Yet it's not the actual day itself but the days leading up to the anniversary date that hurt. By the time "that" day comes, I know I'll be mentally exhausted. People ask, "What are your plans for that day?" But how can I plan for it? All I know is I'll be worthless and unable to focus on anything.*

Like the other mothers, we won't get work done that day; we're not fit to be around people. Instead, I sit on my daughter's bench and just "be" with her. I'll talk to her about her children, her family, and all the things we liked to do together. I wear a piece of her clothing because it's like feeling her next to me. I love doing that. Being physically and emotionally close to her—that's my way of doing it.

SUZIE *As a bereaved parent, I would like to forget or sleep through that day I was told my child was no longer with me. Anniversaries should be days to remember and celebrate. A wedding or anniversary, first day of a new job, or new house—all should be celebrated. I would like to forget the day I said goodbye to my son. I take a candle*

to where my son lies and light it, hoping his light will burn forever.

On my first anniversary day, my sister took me to a tattoo parlor. There, I was tattooed with what should have looked like butterflies flying beside angel wings. They were placed over my forever broken heart.

The two anniversary days I do not celebrate are the day he left me and the day I buried him, which are by no means joyous or happy. They bring tears to my eyes even as I put this on paper. I take these two days off from work every year to sit with my Jamie reminiscing about him, and occasionally family and friends come by and sit with us.

JANIE *I lost my daughter, Missy, on Mother's Day when she was on her way home to enjoy dinner with the family. It was a typical spring day, blue skies and warm temperatures. I had attended church and was surprised when I looked out from the choir loft and saw Missy in attendance with my son and his family. My heart melted with so much pride and love.*

Being Mother's Day, part of the message was about the powerful, never-ending love a mother has for her child. That's when Missy signed to me that she loved me. "I'm the luckiest mother in the world to have three such wonderful children," I thought.

After church, we went to spend time with my mother. After leaving there, I took Missy to get her car and she followed me to the grocery store. As we left the store, Missy asked me if I had picked up her brother's birthday gift. I had forgotten, so I asked her to please pick it up for me. She kissed me goodbye and told me she'd see me at home. Just before she turned into the shopping center, she waved and blew me a kiss. How beautiful she looked at that moment.

At home, I put the groceries away and began getting ready for dinner. The phone rang. It was my husband David, Missy's dad, who told me, "Get down here and hurry." I didn't know where "here" was, but I got in my car and headed out of the subdivision. I knew Missy was in trouble, so the entire way, I screamed, prayed, and tried to make a deal with God.

Then I saw the accident less than a half mile from our home. Missy's car was upside down. David was with her, but I couldn't get to her. I had forgotten my shoes and couldn't climb the fence. I can remember a policeman talking to me, telling me medics couldn't get an airway into her.

David came over to reassure me while the medics finally got Missy out of the car. They let me see her for a second, then whisked her away, in a helicopter, to the hospital.

How could this be happening? I was just with Missy! Everything seemed to move in slow motion but also happening too quickly. I couldn't take it all in. A complete stranger drove us to meet our oldest son, an officer in the city where the hospital was located. We prayed as we sped to the hospital until we got within a mile or so of the building. I told my son to turn the lights and sirens off, knowing Missy was gone. I had felt something wash over my body. I knew she'd left this world. I still can't explain it. I felt changed inside and so alone, knowing my dear child was gone.

I still feel guilty for sending Missy on an errand that day. I'm sure I will carry that guilt with me as long as I live.

Every year, Mother's Day reminds me of what happened on Mother's Day 2004. I experience two days of turmoil— both Mother's Day and May 9th, the day she died.

Sitting in Missy's garden at my church is the one thing that helps me find a bit of peace on this day. It's a place her father and brothers worked hard to create, and she would feel so proud of this garden built in her memory. I know she would.

PATTY: *Crazy. I feel totally crazy anticipating the dreaded anniversary of the passing of my sweet adorable daughter on July 20th. Is this real? I can't believe it is, but it's been six years since her death. How can that possibly be?*

What a perfectly horrible day. I felt sad, angry, lonely, and tired. Oh, how I miss you, Keeley. I try hard to be okay on this day because your brother Hall shares his birthday with the anniversary of your death. Yet on this day in 2015, I could find no joy. I feel bad for Hall, but I feel so much worse because of you.

Oh, how I failed you, my dear. Such anxiety and remorse I feel. What could I have done, should I have done . . . ? If only . . . I don't have any answers, so here I sit in the depression of it all. I see you every day in all that I do. I wear my mask to get through the day. No one understands except those who walk with us on this journey. They, too, know the pain and the sorrow are overwhelming.

Today, Keeley, more than six years after you created the wonderful Rocket Coloring Book, I gave it to Winston, your nephew—a charming, handsome, six-year-old boy ready to start school. He listened patiently as I told your story about Baby Rocket, the toys, the Christmas ornament, and your love for him. Oh, my dear, how you would love him.

He knows you, Keeley. I share your life with him, so he can always remember his Aunt KEE KEE. When I gave Winston the book, Hall stood there with tears streaming. We all miss you so much—daughter, sister, friend.

On that anniversary day, we went to the cemetery to decorate for you. You are remembered, my girl. Dad left another connection bracelet with the angel. Winston left three more bracelets and two Ninja Warriors (one pink and one blue). I left you roses and daisies in a jar decorated with a Life is Good sticker and a connection bracelet around the neck of the jar. The flowers look great, still fresh from the gardening I had done the previous week.

After our walk, we stood back at your side and Winston said a prayer. How sweet it was. He then told me he didn't understand heaven, but I reassured him you are with God, and that we will understand heaven when we arrive there, too. We talked about how joyful it will be when we see you again.

Then we shared a heartfelt moment as I read this poem to Winston and Hall.

> *Do not stand by my grave and weep.*

> *I am not there; I do not sleep.*

I am a thousand winds that blow,

I am the diamond glints on snow.

I am the sunlight on ripened grain,

I am the gentle autumn rain.

When you awaken in the morning hush,

I am the swift uplifting rush

Of quiet birds in circled flight.

I am the soft stars that shine at night.

Do not stand by my grave and cry.

I am not there; I did not die.

—MARY ELIZABETH FRYE, 1932

It has been so important to me that my only grandchild be aware of my daughter's love for him. She was not expected to live until his birthday, but through the Grace of God and his workers, the miracles of medicine gave her life until Winston was eight months old. Oh, how she loved her nephew. Our family talks often about Keeley and all of the wonderful times they would have had together. Aunt Kee Kee will live within his heart forever.

How do I celebrate my son's birthday and commemorate the anniversary of my daughter's death on the same day? That's exactly what this mother has been charged to do—nearly an impossible task for me, especially the emotional me!

However, here I am years later asking, "How did you do it?" I have learned to make this anniversary day a time of great joy and reflection. Both of my children have brought their own special gifts to this world.

Putting my son first on this day is a priority as I continue to celebrate his presence here on earth. Loving and kind, he's a brother who loved his sister and never forgets the joy as well as the pain his birthday brings to our family.

CHAPTER 2

I hope you find your joy!

PATTY: *This was said to me just one year after Keeley died. I still remember how strange the comment felt. I was drowning in my grief, hardly functioning, trying to only exist day by day, and this woman talks about joy!*

What joy? What *is* joy?

The dictionary defines joy as the "emotion of great delight or happiness caused by something exceptionally good or satisfying; feeling of great pleasure and happiness." Really!! How in the world will I ever find *that* joy? I have lost my greatest treasure in this life, my child. What could possibly bring me joy?

Only recently have I re-examined this statement. If I need to find my joy, then I certainly have lost it along the way. So after years of pondering the statement "*I hope you find your joy,*" I know I will never find the kind of joy I had with my daughter on earth, but I can find joy in my memories of her. So my message is simply this: "*Lost in my sorrow, drowning in my grief, looking to you for some relief!*"

WHAT TO SAY
WHEN YOU DON'T
KNOW WHAT
TO SAY

These awkward but common statements and questions can trigger a world of grief for bereaved mothers. In Part II, we share our advice on what to say instead.

You're doing great

You're not the same

I don't want to mention your child because it will make you cry

You are so strong

Be glad you have other children

You're not the first mother who has lost a child

My child almost died, so I know how you feel

Time heals all wounds

Your child wouldn't want you to feel this way

I wouldn't survive if I lost one of my children

Everything happens for a reason

I can't imagine this happening to me

I lost my pet so I can sympathize with you

Dying is a natural part of life

What are the details of the death?

Would you have had your child if you knew?

I guess you are relieved

Did you have a good mother's day?

CHAPTER 3

You're doing great (aka "the mask")

" You're doing so well!"

Boy, does hearing that make us raise our eyebrows. If they only knew the turmoil going on inside. Don't people realize we are *not* who we seem to be now? Nor are we who we were *before*. We make ourselves appear normal by wearing our masks each day.

The mask worn for the benefit of others takes effort to put on. Every day, donning this mask represents a new struggle. Before facing others, we must compose ourselves and force a smile, adjusting our mindset for the next situation.

Grief is not something human beings can put aside easily. However, people in our world can only handle so much of our grief. So they are ready for us to put it aside. Yet we ourselves are the ones who get put aside.

Yes, we fear being alone, but it's also *so much effort* to be around people. Each occasion—whether it's work, gatherings, parties, dinners out, shopping, even funerals—requires immense effort to ensure the mask is in place. We become great pretenders in public, striving to keep our secret contained in private.

To show a side that people aren't used to seeing makes them uncomfortable. Because of that, others may shy away from us, avoid us. Their response to odd behavior or uncomfortable words is to keep moving away. This distance causes even more hurt because we can't explain ourselves to them easily. Instead of tuning in to our reasoning, we are driven by our emotions. That's why we adjust our mask to fit the occasion.

Honestly, telling us how great we're doing makes us clench inside. We think, "You have no idea what hell I live in every day." By saying, "You're doing great," you affirm that on the outside, we've done a fine job of covering our misery. But it's only the mask. Those who have continued to support and comfort us through this grief journey receive our thanks; they know outside appearances disguise the pain and turmoil in our hearts and minds.

Thankfully, over time, the harshness of the pain softens. Some days we feel better, but still not great. We are grateful for those days and hope they increase in number. We're doing the best we can. We simply need to explain our feelings and have a good cry.

JOAN E: *The best thing someone did was sit down beside me on the sidewalk while we both bawled like babies. No words, no trying to "fix" anything.*

Sometimes we let out a big long sigh. That helps! A heavy sigh releases pressure from our grieving. And while sighing is a way of communicating, deep breathing releases our stress. This forces us to "get a grip" so we can rejoin a moment or a conversation. Reach out to us. Sigh with us. Cry with us.

What could you say instead of *"You're doing great"*? Try this:
> **"I realize you appear to be great on the outside, but I understand that's likely masking what you feel on the inside. It's okay to cry, get angry, or break down."**

CHAPTER 4

You're not the same

Why would we be the same now? Every dynamic of our lives is different, both physically and emotionally. Hopes and dreams of the future have been stripped away from us. The blessings we've enjoyed and those yet to come have all changed. We are left with only visions of what should and could have been. Thus, our perspective of life is forever changed.

Others remember our children's lives up to the time of their deaths, but our memories don't stop there. We're still imagining what should have been: vacations, jobs, children, grandchildren. Yet "what should have been" has vanished, and this haunts us continually. Events such as birthdays, weddings, shopping, holidays, and family gatherings deliver an acute awareness of our children's absence. Because we crave all remembrances of them, this becomes a paradox.

As bereaved mothers, our psychological trauma provides a gateway to physical manifestations. When someone in a cast is noticeably injured, helping that person is expected and appreciated. When the cast comes off, we assume they are healed.

But our cast of grief never comes off. It always weighs us down. We are treated with compassion until people think it's time for our cast to be taken off. They don't realize this cast will never be removed. It holds pain that's forever invisible.

Looking *outwardly* healed makes us appear okay in others' eyes. They tell us about a "new" normal. However, normality is illusive. We want to maintain the same life and relationships as before. But normalcy can be too much of a challenge.

Continuing to be "the same" is no longer an option. Family dynamics—changed! The roles we play—gone! So where do we fit into our new roles?

With our perspective of life changed, others' expectations of us also have to shift, too. Preserving old relationships becomes challenging for us. We ask for forgiveness for not being the wife, the mother, the daughter, the grandmother, the relative or friend we used to be. During this new and foreign phase, we ask for your patience and understanding. Allowing bereaved mothers to talk about feelings they're experiencing can help them to go forward.

What could you say instead of *"You're not the same"*?
"Such a deep loss must have changed so many aspects of your life that nothing will ever seem the same. Know that I will always be the same ole me who's here for you."

CHAPTER 5

I don't want to mention your child because it will make you cry

No. No. No. We *want* you to talk about them. We bereaved mothers want to speak about our children.

The tears we shed are tears of joy in remembrance. Even though we need to get up from the table and leave, we still want to hear our children's stories. We need to know you have not forgotten them, that they're still in our lives and our conversations. It's welcoming to hear people include them in their conversations. These words are like crumbs of love that lead us to a better place.

Let us point out that some mothers may close themselves up in a world where they don't want to hear or see anything about their child. You may have to test the waters by putting in a toe first. That way, you can feel out how they may react to the mention of their child's name. Yet, this is rare.

JOAN E *If I say "Cindy would have liked that," people gasp. Yes, it's okay to talk about them; we love hearing about our children. Although we may cry, we cherish the sound of their names. We want you to know they continue to live in our hearts.*

PATTY *Sometimes memories fall out of our eyes as tears that simply bring hope to our hearts. Please give back to us by sharing our children's lives through your friendship, stories, hugs, memories, and love that we may continue to live in them.*

JOAN E *When a guest brought a bottle of wine to dinner, I mentioned it was one of my daughter's favorites. She shrank and said, "Oh, should I not have brought it?" My response was, "I'm absolutely delighted you did bring it. When we finish your wine, we'll open mine. But first, let's all toast my daughter."*

Just because we buried our children doesn't mean we buried them from our minds. We love it when you bring our child's favorite things— wine, cookies, chocolate syrup, macaroni and cheese, whatever—to a gathering. It feels good for someone to share stories and memories about our children. For example, one friend had a bracelet that belonged to the child of a bereaved mother. She didn't know whether to keep it or give it to the mother. Our advice: Offer it to her saying how much it meant to you but you thought it would mean more to the mom. Let her decide to keep it herself or give you the treasure.

What could you say instead of *"I don't want to mention your child because it will make you cry"*? Try this:

"I am thinking about you and your child." *Any memories or mentions of the loved one is always welcome, so feel free to share.*

CHAPTER 6

You are so strong

The strongest tree falls the hardest.

Understand that all our strength has been drained away. We are exhausted from trying to look strong when we feel as weak as kittens. We are propped up by various crutches. Knock those away and we land on our knees, reduced to limp spaghetti and unable to rise to our feet. Weakness and frailty coming from formerly unshakeable people frightens others. It frightens us as well.

The thread of grief intertwines in everything we do. For example, going through an illness without your child is hard. Aren't our children supposed to be here to take care of us? The first time we get in our cars and they aren't with us, it feels unfair. Cry heaves (not dry heaves) follow our thoughts, and we cry until we have no tears left.

Our damaged foundations of strength must be rebuilt one piece at a time, yet it's a puzzle with one monster piece missing.

We're expected to put everything back together when it can never be whole.

We are different people because we're missing a sense of security and trust. Hurt and loneliness have changed us. And grieving alone so we can appear strong to others can make us bitter. Your presence and love provide a calming effect we crave.

What could you say instead of "*You are so strong*"?

"Even though strength is one of your best points, I know it's hard to be strong right now. I'm here for you to lean on anytime. I will support you as you grieve this loss. I have an open heart and time to listen."

CHAPTER 7

Be glad you have other children

This comment begs the question, "Which child would *you* choose to lose?"

We may have other children, but they cannot replace the child we've lost. It's not like a flat tire on your car—no problem; you still have three perfectly good tires to get home on, right? Every one of our children is irreplaceable.

Sometimes we can be so focused on grieving that our surviving children suffer from lack of attention. Then again, we may be so dependent on our surviving children that we smother them. So please help me remember my surviving children while I'm in the depths of my grief. You may even offer to take them to a movie or dinner and free up some of my time.

What could you say instead of *"be glad you have other children"*?

> **"I know no child is replaceable, but I hope having your surviving children around you helps in easing the pain of your loss."**

CHAPTER 8

You're not the first mother who has lost a child

Yes, but I am the first mother who has lost MY child.

We realize a zillion parents have lost children. We wonder how they got through it because, at this point, we see no way to survive. Each child is the life and soul of every parent.

Yes, it happens to other people, but they are not just "other people." They are *us*. So we look to these "others" for advice on how to relieve our pain. We know they go to bed every night unable to shut their eyes from painful thoughts of their child or from waking up in the middle of the night feeling panic. Every morning they rise with their child's name in their hearts and minds. They constantly struggle to get through the day because the knot in their stomachs and the pain in their hearts never ceases.

Knowing others have struggled and kept going does not, in our minds, lessen the hurt or make us feel braver. Still, telling us about others who have lost a child can give us encouragement. It lets us know how hard they fought but eventually got on with their lives. Perhaps we will find a way to have a life without our child—someday.

What could you say instead of "*You're not the first mother who has lost a child*"? Try this:

> **"I know mothers who have lost their children and how much they grieved. I also know bereaved mothers who struggled but eventually got on with their lives. That has made me aware of what a fight this is for you. You will continue to be in my thoughts."**

CHAPTER 9

My child almost died, so I know how you feel

If you said this, you only had a clue about how it might feel to lose a child. That sickness in your stomach—that sharp pain in your chest—were temporary. The urge to "lose your lunch" happened in that moment, then it went away.

Our moments of terror stay with us. Multiple times a day we feel that tightness in our chest as an image or thought comes to us. Watching our children die is haunting. The pain, weakness, tears—they never leave.

Today, your child is living his or her life while our children won't experience another day. We can't see them, smell them, or hear them. We hope you never know how that feels.

But if your child did have a close brush with death, please do not tell us God was watching over *your* child. We know God was watching over our child, too, as He watches over all children. God did not choose.

What could you say instead of "*My child almost died, so I know how you feel*"? Try this:

> **"My child had a close brush with death, which was terrifying enough. There can be no comparison to actually losing a child. I'm here to support you."**

CHAPTER 10

Time heals all wounds

Rose Kennedy may have expressed this sentiment best when she said, "It has been said that 'time heals all wounds.' I do not agree. The wounds remain. In time, the mind, protecting its sanity, covers them with scar tissue and the pain lessens. But it's never gone."

Given time, yes, most physical wounds do heal. Surgeons perform kidney transplants every day. They can replace an amputated limb with a prosthesis or repair a diseased heart. But the healing we need cannot be repaired even with a new heart. Our emotional wound cuts so deep, neither medical science nor time can make it go away.

This open wound never closes. And just when it seems to heal, something comes along to dig into that wound—a memory, an event, a comment, an action, a word starts the time clock all over again. That scab begins the healing process anew. The scar tissue may thicken, but it's always penetrable.

Realize that thoughts of our children and the pain of losing them are never far from the surface. The outside might look strong, but inside the festering continues.

The expected length of the grief journey throws people off. Some people say we've grieved long enough. For Janie, who has grieved eleven years, the sorrow of losing her child has softened, but it never disappears.

Yes, the hurting gets easier as we tolerate the pain and hide it better. Triggers of everyday life can suddenly bring back the pain, requiring us to realize it's to be expected. For us, it's not about how long we've had wounds; rather, it's about how long we've lived *without another wound.*

Our experience of losing a child has shattered us to the core of our being. Piece by piece, we strive to put our lives back together. However, we will never return to the same people we were before losing our child—nor do we want to. A plate that's been shattered will never be the same, even after meticulous gluing and repair work. Nor will we.

Do not expect that one day, preferably sooner than later, we'll return to our former selves. As bereaved mothers, we are exposed to the depth of our souls. There is nothing we have, ever had, or lost that will have such a profound effect as the trauma of losing our child.

As time passes, the grief may soften but it remains deep in our hearts.

What could you say instead of "*Time heals all wounds*"?
Try this:

> *"I hope in time your pain and grief will soften. Knowing it will take time, I stand beside you for the long haul."*

CHAPTER 11

Your child wouldn't want you to feel this way

Then people say, "Your child would *want* you to be happy!"

We know this is true, but here's the problem. We don't know how to be happy *without* our child. Carrying a sorry case of survivor's guilt, it's impossible to feel *any* happiness for a long time.

We truly want to live our lives as our children would like if they were still here. But so much has changed. We no longer fit into our families' lives. Seeing everyone moving on, we feel pushed to live in a way we cannot—without them. We are forever blocked from the old life. *Understand that happiness will take time to return to our lives, so be tolerant with us.*

Sometimes, seeing others being happy with their families drains our emotions. We hunger for that interaction. Other times, we experience sadness seeing parents criticize their child for small things. We only wish we had their problems. We ask for your sensitivity about our problems.

What could you say instead of "*Your child wouldn't want you to feel this way*"? Try this:

> **"Know that your pain is shared, and I have many fond memories of your child." Tell us how much happiness our child brought to you. Sharing memories will help ease our pain and allow happiness to creep back into our lives.**

CHAPTER 12

I wouldn't survive if I lost one of my children

There are no parents who wouldn't go to their graves *with* their child or *for* their child.

Few realize the time we've spent with elbows on knees holding cheeks that are wet from the flow of tears. Few know the time we've moaned and asked God, "Why, why, why?" while wishing we could have traded *our* lives for *theirs*. We can stand in the shower alone with solitary thoughts of our child while aimlessly spraying the wall. When we step out, we're reluctantly forced to rejoin the world.

Many times, our minds tell us to join our children, but our physical bodies force us to move on. We eat the next meal, drink the next glass of water, and move forward one step at a time. Yet we know they will never do these simple things again. Because our children were a part of our "being," when they're gone, a part of us is buried with them. Thus we carry the immense guilt of surviving them. Our grief and guilt can fester into depression and intolerable pain—at times examining suicide as an option.

An article in *Psychology Today* titled "When a Parent Loses a Child" (February 4, 2013) states: "Producing greater stress than dealing with the death of a parent of a spouse, a child's death is especially traumatic because it is often unexpected as well as being in violation of the usual order of things in which the child is expected to bury the parent. The emotional blow associated with child loss can lead to a wide range of psychological and physiological problems including depression, anxiety, cognitive and physical symptoms linked to stress, marital problems, increased risk of suicide, pain and guilt. All of these issues can persist long after the child's death and may lead to diagnosed psychiatric conditions such as complicated grief disorder which can include many symptoms similar to posttraumatic stress disorder. Parents who had lost a child had shorter life spans than non-bereaved parents. The study researchers raise several possibilities including unresolved grief and long-term PTSD. Loss of meaning in one's life and the biological impact of severe prolonged stress were also factors."

However, people like us are needed in this life on earth. We have surviving children, husbands, parents, and others to be with, so we focus whatever strength we have on loving those around us.

Remember, it is not a matter of *if* it's going to happen. It's about *when* and *to whom* losing a child will happen next. We will be there for them, as we wish you to be here for us.

The most valuable thing you can provide is your gift of time, patience, and love as we take one baby step at a time. We pray that we can find more stable footing and stay afloat through this trauma.

What could you say instead of "*I wouldn't survive if I lost one of my children*"?

> *"I feel saddened by your loss of _____ (name) and can't fathom the pain you're going through. I feel the depth of love I have for my children, so I know the effort to survive without them would be overwhelming."*

Note: Mentioning the child's name makes if feel as if you're *entering into the pain* with the mother rather than just talking about it.

CHAPTER 13

Everything happens for a reason

And that reason is . . . ?

Our children were good, generous, loving individuals. They were not taken from us so the world would be a better place to live. Why couldn't it have been someone more deserving of death? There is *never* a good enough reason our children were taken.

Could anything good come from the loss of a child? Perhaps by bringing awareness of the horrific pain we endure accomplishes that for this group of authors. The bonding we experienced has transformed the four of us. Together, we hashed through a lot of our emotions, which would not have happened otherwise. And when all four shed tears at the same time, that breaking point emotionally drained us for an entire day.

Going forward, if only one person claims he or she has learned from this book's advice and now regards bereaved mothers in a more understanding way, our purpose has been served. Our journey has been worth the stories, memories, breakdowns, disagreements, and rivers of tears. Did it have to take four children dying to get to that point? No, we'd all prefer having the ignorance of our pain continue than losing a child.

What could you say instead of *"Everything happens for a reason"*? Try this:

> **"It goes beyond reason for any child to be taken from a mother. There was certainly no good reason to lose yours."**

CHAPTER 14

I can't imagine this happening to me

Neither can we. Even when confronted with their deaths, the finality is still unimaginable. We watched them through the dying process until we realized there was no turning back. We held out hope until the last minute because, no, we couldn't imagine it. We embraced our loved ones so tight because we refused to see reality. After their deaths, our imagination really kicked in. We "saw" our children everywhere—in stores, in cars, in crowds, and in our minds.

No, we still can't imagine our children being gone. We imagine them still in our lives every day because their images bring them back to us.

No, you will never imagine the pain we endure because until the moment your child dies, no amount of imagination can prepare you for the hurt and the nightmare that becomes your life. So imagining our grief does us no good. Rather, call with a kind word or offer a shoulder to lean on. And don't expect the bereaved to call you; they simply aren't able.

What could you say instead of *"I can't imagine this happening to me"*? Try this:

> **"I could never imagine the pain you're feeling. I want to be here for you to help carry the load. If there's a way I can assist during this indescribable time of pain, I will be there for you."**

CHAPTER 15

I lost my pet so I can sympathize with you

We love our animals. Our children love their pets, and we have cried together when we lost them. But to compare your animal's death to a child's death can't be comprehended. Our children are not critters; they are our bloodlines. They were a piece of us. They were contributing members of society. Some had children depending on them. They were good people.

When a piece of our future has been stripped from us, know this: *We don't want to hear about your pet.*

What could you say instead of *"I lost my pet so I can sympathize with you"*? Try this:

> **"I have lost loved ones and pets I've loved dearly, but never a child. Just thinking about losing my pet makes me cry. I realize I can never fully understand the depth of your pain."**

CHAPTER 16

Dying is a natural part of life

There is nothing natural about one's child dying before the mother who gave that baby life. As mothers, we feel strong urges to protect our young—like a rabbit that chases a snake away so it doesn't harm its baby. The rabbit might have won that battle, but we four moms lost ours.

No one is supposed to have a conversation with a child about that child's impending death. It's *un*natural. Some of our children had a level of acceptance in knowing they were dying, yet they showed concern with the living. "Mom, it's okay" or "Mom, I want you to be okay," they said. And we'd tell them, "We'll be okay."

How did this death discussions flip-flop on us? They trusted us to make the right decisions in the future for them. They told us we'd know what they'd want. Giving us this permission was intended to give us comfort. Yet, there's nothing natural about watching your child prepare for death or witnessing a last breath. No mother would not have traded *her* life for the life of her child.

It's not natural for the child to die before the parent, so it gives us no comfort to be reminded we will all die anyway.

What could you say instead of "*Dying is a natural part of life*"? Try this:

> *"The death of a child before the parent must bring unbearable pain. It seems so unnatural and unexpected. It's certainly not the natural order of life for any mother to lose her child. My heart goes out to you."*

CHAPTER 17

What are the details of the death?

Just turn on the TV and know sensationalized bad news is always out there. The public has a fascination with the terrible details of a tragedy.

However, the details of our child's death aren't intended to be relived or remembered. We are real people with real lives; we are not news events to be sensationalized. A death is a highly personal, horrific event that's not for gossip or, God forbid, social media posts. Thus anyone's questions, comments, and speculations about the details of death are intrusive, hurtful.

Please respect the nuances of our child's death story. They're ours to share in our own time. We don't want to carry them locked up in our minds forever, but we must feel trusting enough to vent when the time is right.

What could you say instead of *"What are the details of the death?"* Try this:

> *"I know that your final moments together hold a special private place in your heart. However, if you need me to listen, I will be there for you with trustworthy ears."*

CHAPTER 18

Would you have had your child if you knew?

We're dumfounded to hear this cruel question: *If you knew your child would be so ill, would you still have had your child?*

Of course, we would have brought this child into the world. Every moment, hour, day, or year holds cherished memories. We hurt so much because we loved our children so much. Even though the grieving can be unbearable, the joy they brought to our lives fulfilled a special purpose—that is, teaching us the true meaning of love.

As I weep

My Soul to keep

What about the hole

In the middle of my soul?

—JOAN E.

What could you say instead of *"Would you have had your child if you knew?"* Try this:

> *"I know that, no matter the condition of any child at birth or at death, your child is always the most special part of your life and loved by you as only a mother could. Let me reassure you that our child mattered and the world is a better place because of that."*

CHAPTER 19

I guess you are relieved

This continues to haunt. Even though some of our children suffered for months, I assure you there was never a feeling of relief when they died. We would have taken care of our children no matter the condition of their bodies, just to have them with us. Another hour, another day, would have brought us relief. Mothers become selfish when it comes to their children; we'll do anything to keep them with us.

We never wished for them to die. We only wanted to extend their time, hoping for a miracle that never came. True, there is no pain for them now and, yes, they suffered. And although we're glad the suffering is over, we gain no relief knowing they are gone. None.

What could you say instead of *"I guess you are relieved"*? Try this:

> **"I'm so sorry that your child had to go through so much. But with you by his/her side, I'm sure you made it better during this difficult time."**

CHAPTER 20

Did you have a good Mother's Day?

~⊱⊰~

A re you kidding me? Yes, people have actually asked that question!

Thank goodness that hearing "Mom, you are still my mom" from a surviving child jerks us back to the moment. We are still mothers to the rest of our children, and Mother's Day is for our other children, too. Still, holding it together is difficult.

There is no name for a bereaved mother. Widow, widower, or orphan implies a death, but no known word is appropriate enough for us. We are nameless. Departed mothers are honored at a Mother's Day memorial, but what about the mothers who've lost children? They experience a double whammy.

It seems ironic that, on a day of honor, we feel that much is missing—except unwanted reminders. Some bereaved moms don't go to work the day after Mother's Day because people talk about what they did on that holiday. Janie lost her daughter

Missy in a car accident on Mother's Day, so all day she feels panicky reliving the experience and fearing tragedy will strike again. We look forward to this day of marked sadness being over.

What could you say instead of *"Did you have a good Mother's Day?"* Try this:

> *"It must be difficult to hear about the awesome day other mothers had with their children. I acknowledge your loss and would share a special memory about your child who died. Would you like to share yours?"*

PART III

BEREAVED MOTHERS: WHAT YOU CAN DO TO SOFTEN YOUR OWN GRIEF

CHAPTER 21

Yes, we're fine

Yes, we are fine! Or so it seems to everyone. After the loss of a child, people finally get brave enough to ask how we are. For the most part, we don't know what to say because we don't *know* how we are. We struggle to answer every simple question.

JANIE *We have a hurt so deep that it's impossible to explain, which makes surviving this tragedy somewhat doubtful. So our easiest truthful reply is "FINE."*

But "FINE" holds a different meaning to us, depending on the day.

Our Good-Day Version	Our Bad-Day Version
Frustrated	Furious
Irritated	Insecure
Numb	Neurotic
Exhausted	Emotional

Frustrated = Failing our children; not protecting them when we felt they needed us most.

Irritated = We become irate when others don't "get" us. Will telling us to put on a smile and do something fun to make us feel better? Impossible.

Numb = The shock, the emotions, and the hurt make us oblivious to the outside world.

Exhausted = Grieving is insurmountable work. There is no rest for the grieving mind.

These are the meanings for the bad day FINE:

Furious = at everyone for not understanding.

Insecure = Not sure we even want to see another day.

Neurotic = Knowing the depression is taking our sanity away.

Emotional = Tear up when I try to talk; answering the phone is out of the question today.

When friends and family members ask, giving a "FINE" reply with its double meaning gets both sides off the hook.

CHAPTER 22

Throwing eggs!

It's difficult to express the mixture of emotions we feel as a bereaved mother when our child is no longer with us. These strong new emotions of anger, hopelessness, and terrible loneliness confuse us. We desperately need a break from this nightmare if only for a brief moment.

JANIE *I have a special way of venting my frustration: Throwing eggs. As I feel the egg leaving my hand and the sound of the splat against the pavement or fence, true relief follows! For a brief moment, I feel in control and have a glimmer of hope for continuing with my life. I even took eggs to my niece, Cindy, while she was in the hospital as a cancer patient. Her mom held up a trash can like a basketball hoop, then she threw the egg, missed the can, and hit the wall. It was well worth the clean up to hear Cindy laugh.*

When there are no words, throw eggs!

CHAPTER 23

Turning to healthcare providers

We greatly appreciate those caregivers who have treated us and our children with compassion because they made the journey less frightening. Yet our research shows a division in attitude among our children's healthcare providers.

Many physicians who work at children's hospitals especially are among the most caring and compassionate in medicine. This is also true of the many other healthcare providers in a hospital's oncology or cancer wings. One impressive response came when we saw a gynecologist weep with a huge volume of feeling after she'd learned about a child's passing. What a tender, intimate occasion.

However, those caregivers who go about their business dispassionately fall into a whole different category. We wish no one the misfortune of being in their care. Our advice is to make sure the medical people you work with can be trusted and show respect for the situation. If they don't, then get a second opinion, and if they discourage you in doing this, dismiss them as care providers for your loved one.

> JOAN E *A surgeon leaned over my daughter's bed while she slept, or so I thought. Then she said, "Well, doesn't she know about her prognosis?" I perceived that the doctor didn't care about her as if she'd said, "She's going to die anyway, so why bother." This tells me professionals dealing with death situations should be given more training in grief counseling. After all, the physical aspects of patients dying isn't the only care needed.*
>
> *This doctor's abrupt reminder of my daughter's short future led me to a middle-of-the-night walk through the hospital corridors. Seeing they were vacant, I slid down a wall to cry in private. When I looked up, I was against the "gift of life" wall for organ donors. I'd seen it before. But this time, as I looked closely, the plaque with Missy Fields' name on it was staring down at me.*
>
> *I knew then that my daughter would be holding her cousin's hand before long.*

Greatly appreciate those caregivers who treat you and you children with compassion, dignity, and respect.

CHAPTER 24

Dealing with "God issues"

Naturally, you want to hold on to whatever higher power is in your life to give you comfort. Some bereaved mothers grow closer to God than they ever were. They've learned to depend on God for strength and support through their grief.

Yet whether someone believes in God or not, the suffering after the loss of a child is horrendous. Our faith can be so quickly shattered; our losses left unexplained. People try by saying such phrases as "God created another Angel," or "Your child is sitting on the right hand of God" or "Your children are in a better place" or "God will never give you more than you can handle" or "God had a plan."

When people make these God-related statements, they're searching for words of comfort to share. We understand that. But these phrases perplex us and offer little consolation. Instead of being beneficial, a bereaved mother's faith might be "on trial" because she's already struggling with her beliefs. Any of these "God" statements can tax a mother's confused mind.

Know this: Making statements that attempt to rationalize our children's deaths through God provides no comfort to some of us. What may result in a lifelong journey of rebuilding our faith can't be summed up in a simple catch phrase.

We are all different. One grieving mother might go right back to church after losing her child, while another fights internally to find her way back to God's house. Still another grieving mother might have no desire to return to church several years after her child's death. Mostly, it's due to the overwhelming stress of facing so many people who know her story at once.

> JOAN E. *It took me a year and a half to go back to my church family who'd never let go of me. I will always love them for that. But I couldn't return to services because I knew the congregation would say The Lord's Prayer. This is the prayer my daughter and I said over and over while she was in intense pain during her cancer treatment. I sensed I'd break down into tears when it was said at church.*
>
> *Then about two years after Cindy's burial, I stood at her gravesite with two church leaders. I felt a shiver go through me as they said The Lord's Prayer aloud, and then suddenly I felt okay to again say it at church.*

Faith and Grief

Historically, grief has been an inward battle within an expected time frame. Young ones dying was the norm and hardworking people had to continue with life, so their grief for their loved ones got swept under the rug. Their grieving took place behind closed doors. During this time of grief, women hid their sadness under their cloaks, in their homes, or in the fields.

Today, life expectancy has increased significantly. U.S. National Vital Statistics pegged the average life expectancy at 78.8 years in 2014 (National Vital Statistics Report, Volume 65, Number 4, June 30, 2016). Our grieving has taken a modern turn. According to the *British Journal of Medicine,* grieving parents have life spans that are shorter than average. For example, the suicide rate for bereaved parents is much higher than the norm. They might come face to face with insanity, suicide, alcoholism, or drug abuse—or simply hide from the world. (See this blog post by Jody Glynn Patrick for more statistics and observations: *https://jodyglynnpatrick.com/2012/11/18/your-child-died-too-soon-chances-are-greater-then-that-you-will-too/*)

In essence, bereaved mothers are standing on the edge of a cliff believing the only way to quell their pain is to jump. The pressure and the triggers keep piling up to make the misery unbearable. Sometimes, yes, we feel God gave us more than we could handle. We pray we can hold it together for just one more dinner, one more meeting, or one more day.

As we wallow in self-pity, people need to know how fragile we feel. *We* don't even know how fragile we are. We feel so alone in the wilderness of our minds.

Remember, we are driven by emotions, not reasoning. Living feels pointless without our child. Fortunately, we can be pulled back. We realize we are needed in other areas and have to go on. Surviving children, grandchildren, parents, and others are hurting as well. Slowly, we poke our heads out of the darkest caves of our mind to be there for them. Was this more than we could handle? Almost.

What could you say instead?

"I know you have a lot to handle. I'm there for you. I love you and I care. Let me help you take steps toward handling this painful situation the best you can. If possible, give me some direction to help give you back some control."

Role of Clergy

We have discovered firsthand how ill-prepared clergy, doctors, and other professionals are in dealing with grief. We learned that, surprisingly, there's a lack of grief counseling given to the clergy, and many pastors concurred. Typically, they are *not* equipped to handle our grief. Yes, they can assure us our children are in a safe place but are not prepared for the one-on-one support mothers need. It seems only experienced chaplains or clergy can deal with us.

Seminaries and colleges teach the business end of running a church, directing the training toward sustaining a church following and dealing with the masses. Most clergy deal with grief from the Bible or the pulpit. They are not prepared to help us deal with the pain or compassion we need. Several clergy have even mentioned that giving hugs or advice could be a liability for them in today's world. When we turn to them seeking comfort, they rarely understand the long road we travel.

One bereaved mother had lost three children after the oldest shot himself and his siblings. The family's pastor came to this mother requesting she not have a funeral service that included all three children. Why? This church didn't think it was proper to mourn them together because of the violent actions of her one son. She responded, "But the oldest was my child, too, and I love all my children."

Such a sad story. To a mother, a child is a child. We love all our children unconditionally. And every child deserves our love and forgiveness.

Blessed by God

The four of us gain peace as we believe our children are with God.

God has blessed us with the gift of our children, and we are grateful. But to give us this gift and then take it away seems totally irrational. How could this be His plan? How can we feel blessed when we actually feel punished?

At some point, we come to realize that *God* didn't take our children; the cancer, illness, accident, suicide, overdose, even murder took them. Yet, we had all prayed to God to answer our prayers and deliver miracles. Rebuilding our lives without our children or our faith is a monumental task emotionally. Any source of comfort, whether it's derived from a religious affiliation or not, is good.

PART IV

THOSE WHO LOVE
BEREAVED MOTHERS:
HOW TO SOFTEN
THEIR GRIEF

CHAPTER 25

The sorry factor:
when we say the wrong things

Because our thought processes never seem to catch up with reality, we're constantly saying, "I'm sorry. I'm sorry for crying. I'm sorry I can't go. I'm sorry I didn't mean that. I'm sorry . . ."

Frankly, we are tired of being sorry. Throughout this book, we don't express being sorry for anything. Rather, we risk offending our own families and friends as we share insights from our experiences. It's because we want to spare future grieving parents additional suffering from unintentional comments and actions.

Understand that it's a struggle *every day* for us to act normally. Realizing life goes on, we prepare ourselves to appear normal and pretend life is good. Sometimes we can't quite get there, so we say the wrong things or commit mindless actions. The fog in our minds caused by insurmountable stress and grief can make us look and feel weak, even unstable. So simply do this:

Allow us the space to "be" without expecting to hear "I'm sorry."

CHAPTER 26

Taking time off work

THREE days. In the United States, that's how much time is legally given bereaved parents to get over the loss of their child. After three days, we're required to return to work. Imagine the stress: "I lost my son, arranged for his funeral, tried to grasp the loss of him—and I had to do it all in three days." Then compare that to the six weeks mothers are given to bond with their newborns.

Three days off is neither fair nor productive considering there's probably more emotion involved in losing a child as bringing one into the world. Thus, a three-day leave doesn't even represent a beginning. Still feeling numb, bereaved parents aren't equipped to handle the faces, the questions, and the normality of everyone else's lives. That's why the legislation needs to change. Passing a new bereaved parent law would have to address the innate unfairness of this mourning time.

SUZIE *At this devastating time, I considered myself fortunate to take off two weeks by adding vacation days to the three-day bereavement policy. Not once was I asked by my employer if I needed additional time off. Because my son was an adult who didn't live at home, I used that time to gather his belongings. That wasn't easy. I found myself scurrying around instead of taking needed time to grieve for my son.*

With only a couple of days left before I had to return to work, I became nauseated and mentally sick. I anticipated everyone in the office would be giving advice on how to cope with my loss. Go figure; the non-bereaved parents with their happy families are telling me how to go on with a life that I no longer wanted. How could I focus and not stop thinking about my son?

After the death of a son or daughter, there are no platitudes, no Twelve Steps, no medications, no words of wisdom, and no instruction on how to get over it. We have to live a different way for the rest of our lives—and live with the pain.

What could you do?

Push for legislation to extend the number of time-off days allowed for grieving parents when their child dies.

CHAPTER 27

Threads of grief

Threads of grief intervenes in everything we do. When there's an event for your child such as a wedding or a birthday party, hearing stories about that experience can be difficult. The stories can even intensify the loss we feel. For example, if you invite us to your child's graduation party and our child was in that same graduation class, don't be surprised if we use our "out." Celebrating these occasions in others' lives can be impossible. We long for our loved one's touch at every holiday and family gathering.

JOAN E *Thanksgiving is the hardest for me, possibly because it signals the start of the holiday season. On the first Thanksgiving when I was with my husband's family, all I could do was cry. My husband Denny rescued me and we left. The only place we could find open to eat was White Castle, so we had a White Castle Thanksgiving dinner.*

Bear with us as we slowly become more comfortable in these situations. For the sake of our family and our own peace of mind, we want to ease into the flow of life again. Laughing for the first time is a breakthrough moment. Yet the first time a mother enjoys herself, the guilt she feels may be all consuming.

As Janie experienced the day of her daughter's funeral, "idiot" relatives talked to her about a new house, their bright futures, and so on. That kind of thoughtless talk made her retreat to her bedroom. *How could they think about building a future when her daughter was gone?*

> PATTY *"It's hard to go there"* was my husband Berkeley's *comment as I continued with my writing for this book. Yes, it is hard to "go there"— into the prison of grief, cold, heart-wrenching pain, loneliness, and hopelessness with an out-of-control mind asking the "what if's and why's."*
>
> *So why do I write?* To protect my heart. Keep up my guard. Act as if all is well. *The most healing part of writing for this book is letting me be just who I am—critically wounded and forever changed.*

We have times of wondering how everyone can go on when our child is gone. We want to scream, "I am here, and I am hurting!" So we go to our safe place, our home. Some will check on us there; others will write us off. If certain people can't be avoided, that's when the mask comes in.

Anyone who loses a child is drawn to others enduring the same misfortune and we can lean on them for support. That's why all four of us recommend some type of professional help. Like a physical pain that is unbearable, the emotional pain often requires expertise from doctors, psychologists, grief counselors, and if necessary, medication to address the mental anguish. Grief derails the simplest actions while pain eats away at the soul. What can you do?

Be sensitive to the feelings of the bereaved in all situations and encourage them to get the help they need.

CHAPTER 28

Post-traumatic stress disorder

WOW! What a surprise that we have post-traumatic stress disorder!

Fear, shaking, panic, and numbness are just a few symptoms commonly endured along with the grief. Pretending to be normal on the outside fails us when the PTSD takes over. Then, we are anything but normal and fully aware of it.

Just as soldiers at war have experienced and witnessed life-changing dramatic events, so have we. Their emotions have triggers and so do ours. A person, a place, a sound, a smell, or an event can reduce us to a mumbling idiot. Triggers can make us feel sluggish or immobile as if the world has stopped moving. A fog consumes us.

In the beginning, it can be impossible to remain focused on anything except feeling overwhelmed. Our own reactions seem foreign and are oh-so-difficult to rein in. We must appear creepy to others when coherent sentences won't form in our brains and we can't understand logic.

Each one in our foursome of grieving mothers has been diagnosed with PTSD. The triggers are totally different for each of us. People around us don't know *what* is happening or even realize that something *is* happening. They just know they don't want to be around us. Some say, "Just don't think about it," which is *not* possible. The object of the PTSD can possess our minds.

Trust us; we don't *want* to think about it, but we have no option. Knowing we aren't acting normal and receiving funny looks, we amble off, lost in the terror inside our minds.

If soldiers came home from war after having watched their best friends get shot or die in their arms, they might very well develop PTSD. A loud, unexpected noise could instantly take them to a scary place in their minds. Knowing that, would you take those soldiers to a firing range? No.

Similarly, don't be offended if we walk away when situations get difficult. This may be our best option until we work through our triggers over time.

If you're with a bereaved mother who's acting abnormally or appears emotionally distraught, what can you do?

Allow for the possibility of PTSD from a grieving mother. To help settle her nerves and slow her heart rate, talk to her in a calming tone. Walk her away from a triggering situation if you can. Share a private word or signal to prevent irrational behavior. Mostly, talk about the core of the problem, not its result.

Even though we might put you in an uncomfortable situation with our strange actions, helping us makes us forever grateful.

CHAPTER 29

Stepping in too quickly

The space around loved ones who've experienced loss is a sacred space.

Family members need time to heal together. They've traveled a terrible path and now seek healing and grieving as a family. By "stepping in" too quickly into their space, that needed time is taken away. Our crisis brain could see the helpful person as someone trying to replace our loved one. That could lead to pushing the family apart at a time when they should be leaning on one another.

After a death, realize that everyone in the family is emotionally and physically drained—and feeling highly vulnerable. Any intrusion at their weakest moment can cause unnecessary conflict and complication. It can create yet another stressful situation to deal with.

If it's a new social relationship, the situation can be even more confusing for the bereaved mother. Sometimes a quasi-romantic relationship could be perceived as potentially being full blown.

Thus, she could be condemned to an additional heart-wrenching pain while stumbling through already overwhelming grief. Being around the one stepping in can then feel like a hot poker prodding the heart, forcing her to wear a mask even tighter just to handle the situation/person.

Because we are mothers and protectors of our children, this behavior can also seem to disrespect our child's memory. We must be given enough time to start healing. Is there a timeline when someone could safely get closer to the bereaved? No, there's not. But you can help by doing this:

Give family members space. Be helpful and caring, but if you represent a new relationship that could be stressful to anyone; step back. Consider the thoughts and emotions of all involved by showing compassion to hurting family members. They feel vulnerable and overly sensitive, and they're not ready for anything new.

CHAPTER 30

Phantom pain

It is said that if one loses a limb, there's still a feeling of pain or movement in that limb. The loss of our children is like that. We feel them so we reach out to someone who's no longer there. We're expected to accept the unacceptable, but the phantom pain never allows for that. So we continue to limp along.

We want to feel our loved ones as a part of us, but the horror of not having these "missing limbs" can overwhelm us.

PATTY *As my grandson ran through the house, Keeley's brother Hall said, "The only thing missing is Keeley."*

JANIE *While shopping for a wedding gown with my niece Erin, I could feel Missy sitting next to me. She would have not missed this event!*

JOAN E *As if she were standing by my side at her boys'
rodeo, I can hear my daughter Cindy yelling, "Faster,
faster, go, go."*

SUZIE *The day my granddaughter arrived in this world,
my son Chase and I felt Jamie standing with us looking at
his niece Katy. Jamie's presence felt so strong, tears of joy
and sorrow rolled down our faces.*

Please realize that the anguish of losing a child is never far
from the surface. We always feel our loved one's presence.

What could you do?

**Be understanding when we reach for that phantom
companion.**

CHAPTER 31

Sleeplessness

Sleep? Whether our child's loss was from a sudden death or a long-term sickness or injury, sleep evades us. In a hospital situation, who can sleep beyond the fragmented moments of resting our eyes?

We are exhausted before their deaths, yet afterward, sleep still isn't an option. Each night we wonder, "Will I sleep tonight?"

Along with the stress, sleeplessness sets us up for chronic illness. Feeling scared, some of us believe medication is the only way to get through life—one pill to get through the night and another to get through the day. Unfortunately, no amount of medication can take away our nightmares!

Instead of taking prescription drugs, some bereaved mothers deal with these issues by praying to God, meditating, exercising, doing yoga, and more. These strategies help relieve stress and aid sleep with limited success.

Some mothers manage without taking drugs; some hold out longer than others before taking them. In the end, our group of four couldn't find relief in any other form. Still, it's a tough decision to use medications to alter the mind and bring on the sleep we need.

If we appear hound-dog tired, listless, or fatigued, we are! If we appear wired, tense, or aggravated, be patient. It takes a long time for our resources or medications to bring us back to a more normal state of mind.

What could you do?

Give us time to work through our angst, knowing it's an incredibly slow process. Encourage us to find ways to sleep—and heal.

CHAPTER 32

The pain of not knowing

We are stunned to learn about relatives who did not know about our children's struggles or their deaths. How could they not have been informed of such a tragedy? It puts us in the position of having to tell the death story—again and again. Not a preferred or pleasant experience.

Running into people we know closely who haven't been told about this life-changing tragedy is hard to face. The shock is mutual.

What can be done instead?

If you're a bereaved mother or know one, ask family members to inform all close friends and relatives. Making others aware can avoid unhappy encounters that cause heartache.

CHAPTER 33

Honoring children who have passed

To honor those who have died and offset some stress, we suggest doing a project in their memory. Each mother in our group of four has left a lasting memory to honor her child and get outside of herself.

JOAN E *For Cindy, a tree was planted at the cemetery and a bench was placed to sit on. The Chamber of Commerce coordinated a fund-raising drive to raise money for the Humane Society in her name. A lighted sign was donated to the Chamber of Commerce, of which my daughter Cindy was a past president. I love driving by at night to see the glow of the light, which in turn makes my heart glow. Feeling her presence and knowing the impact her life had helps in my recovery.*

PATTY *Keeley's Room in the newly renovated Children's Wing at Crestwood Christian Church in Lexington, Kentucky, was dedicated in 2017. Keeley was an active*

*member of Crestwood, where she experienced the uncon-
ditional love and acceptance of Jesus Christ. In Keeley's
Room, children of all talents and abilities feel welcomed,
loved, and accepted. There, they can learn songs, play
instruments, and express their love of God through music.
By honoring Keeley, we hope to keep her ministry alive
for generations of children to come even though they
never had a chance to know her as we did*

JANIE *Missy was a third-generation member of South
Elkhorn Christian Church in Lexington, Kentucky. She
loved her church and began planning her wedding to be
there when she was only fourteen years old. With the
support of the church members, family members, and
friends, the serene Faith, Hope, and Love Garden was
built on the church grounds. The rock surrounding a
portion of the garden ironically came from our family
farm as well as her cousin Cindy's farm.*

*An advocate for organ donation, Missy's portrait was
featured on the Donate Life Float at the 2011 Rose Bowl
Parade. I continue to be her voice by speaking to groups
about the importance of organ donation.*

PATTY *In the early days of Keeley's illness, she and her
brother Hall bought colorful beaded bracelets that became*

symbols of their love and connection to each other. Keeley and Hall quickly shared those bracelets with others. Before long, ten, then twenty, then fifty people were wearing beaded bracelets to express their support and prayers for Keeley's health and recovery. Within a month, the stores were sold out of the colorful bracelets.

Keeley's dad reassured her he would make more bracelets—as many as she could possibly need. The challenge was on! Her dad, brother, mother, relatives, and friends made hundreds of bracelets. People from coast to coast wore them—doctors, nurses, housekeepers, dietary workers, and patients at the Cincinnati Children's Hospital. They became known as Keeley's connection bracelets—and still are today.

Seven years after Keeley's death, people still ask about my connection bracelet and ask where they can buy one. I gratefully take bracelets from my arm and give them away. It means a lot to me.

SUZIE *After seeing bereaved parents put their heart and soul into a garden to honor their daughter's memory, I felt compelled to do something so my son would never be forgotten. When I went to the cemetery where Jamie lives and told the caretakers, they designated an area for the Garden of Angels. There, all bereaved parents, grandparents, family, and friends would be able to gather*

and remember their loved ones. They also purchase and place benches and memorial bricks with a special person's name on it.

To build this Garden, I raised money through motorcycle poker runs with the help of three biker friends, one who is no longer with us. Another biker stepped up to fill in for him. Friends and relatives also volunteered their time, dedication, and compassion. However, due to the large amount of funds required, instead of creating a garden, we will build a low-maintenance butterfly statue instead to symbolize children who have gone.

Jamie often surprised me with a note and his drawing of beautiful butterflies on the envelopes. Years ago, Jamie and I would collect butterflies and pin them to felt to keep them beautiful. Not long before losing him, he asked me where these butterflies were, but to this day, I haven't been able to locate them. Still, when I see a butterfly, Jamie is reminding me he's always with me.

What could you do?

Suggest and support a project in a lost child's memory—one that will help bring peace to a mother's heart.

CHAPTER 34

We'll take hugs!

Sometimes no words come across in a loud enough voice. Strangers show us more compassion than close friends and relatives because they aren't emotionally attached. Family members too must heal, and by distancing themselves from us, they can concentrate on their own healing.

The best comfort often comes from a child who doesn't worry about saying the wrong or right thing. Children simply speak what's in their hearts. And getting a hug from a concerned child is absolutely the best.

If adults could ever revert back to showing this kind of unconditional love, our grieving process could be much more bearable.

JOAN E *I was never a touchy-feely person, but now I will take all the hugs I can get.*

What could you do?

Give hugs often! Also saying "I have no words" is a highly powerful way to show your concern.

CHAPTER 35

Yes, we have quirks

Here's a litany of quirks you might witness from bereaved mothers:

- Can't read obituaries any more
- Can't pick up pennies for good luck again
- Can't use certain words even if it means losing a Scrabble® game
- Can't watch familiar TV shows
- Can't listen to the same radio station
- Can't look at an open casket
- Can't stand to read the word "dead"
- Can't look toward the sky
- Can't go to funerals
- Can't watch the news
- Can't answer the phone
- Can't shop certain places

- Can't wear perfume since I lost my daughter. She would turn up her nose at the overpowering aroma.

- Can't save the good stuff for the special occasions any more

- Can't walk down the aisle that has Mother's Day Cards

What could you do to soften the grief?

Show you accept our quirks and don't judge us for them.

CHAPTER 36

Resetting priorities

What's it like to feel like a mere shadow of a person?

JANIE *As I hear all the laughter in a crowded, I think,
"You people have no idea one person among you is a
mere shadow of a person." The real me left when my sweet
Missy departed from this earth. Ironically, I feel isolated
when surrounded by others.*

*I no longer feel whole. My heart is shattered. My love of
life has made a huge detour. I feel guilty for not being the
Mom and Grandma I once was. I'm saddened that my
grandchildren don't know who I was before Missy left.
How heartbreaking they don't know their Aunt Missy
except from our stories and photos.*

*If normal people talk about their children and we mothers
keep quiet about ours, it hurts our hearts. Yet when
we tell a story about a child we've lost, some ignore our*

statements or simply run. This slap in the face makes us feel like our children don't matter.

The bereaved and normal don't "get" each other. I don't sweat the small stuff when they do. I feel agitated when they complain about what they have to do for their children. Oh, I'd love the chance to do anything for Missy.

Do I appear as shallow to them as some appear to me? Probably. My perspective of life has changed and the loss of my child has reset my priorities. So I withdraw from the drama and avoid the small stuff. It's no longer important to me.

What can you do to soften the grief?

Invite conversations about the lost children, showing you know they still matter!

CHAPTER 37

Sharing our pain

We are near paralyzed in grief and unable to step out of ourselves. People often make themselves feel better by saying what comforts *them*, not necessarily what comforts *us*. People who say "I don't know if I can handle this" or "I don't want to see them like this" or "I want to remember them the way they were" are trying, but these statements do nothing to ease a mother's pain.

What sacrifices would help? For one, don't say, "Call me when you are ready." *We are never ready.* That means we may never get your support. A better way is to coax us out of our shells to become a part of the world again. We do appreciate your invitations and offers, even if we turn them down. If we attend an event, it's best to have an "out"—a separate car or a rescue person in case we need to escape.

In time, we hope to recover pieces of ourselves and share our lives again. For now, just share our pain.

Patty *Keeley was blessed with many Angels in her life. Relatives, friends, professionals, acquaintances, and even strangers shared my daughter's cancer journey. She had a happy-go-lucky attitude and a personality with a magnetic force.*

Only after Keeley died did I realize all the people who surrounded her with love and support were really Keeley's Angels. I thought they were my angels (and they were to an extent), but I didn't know they would mostly go away. Hospice workers had closed the case; clergy were back attending to the living; friends and family moved on with their lives. Yes, a few people stayed in touch, but very few.

Life goes on—at least their lives go on. Herein lies the difference. Time has simply stopped for the bereaved.

Patty *My husband's dear 90-year-old Aunt Leslie returned from a luncheon with her college sorority sisters. The new housemother read her name and said, "Did you know your son Toll asked me out in high school?" Aunt Leslie was surprised and delighted to hear a story about her son, who had died at the age of 18 in 1968. This was such a great moment to know her dear son had not been forgotten, even after 48 years.*

SUZIE *Since the day I was told my son Jamie was no longer with us, I shut everyone out of my life. When I start to speak about my son, tears flow, which is why I choose not to share my thoughts.*

The one person I shouldn't have shut out was my son Chase, Jamie's baby brother. Chase had not only lost his brother, his idol, and his best friend; he lost his mother as well—all in the same day. It remained that way for a good year or longer. In fact, Chase had been with me when the physicians delivered the news. I remember looking at him and then back at the doctors. After that, I completely lost it. I just wanted to be with my Jamie.

My surviving son witnessed me become crushed by grief. At the same time, he became invisible to me. So did my husband, sisters, mother, and friends. I wouldn't allow anyone in my heart with the exception of bereaved mothers, who suddenly became my friends.

Today, I would give different advice to newly bereaved mothers—that is, share your grief by expressing your feelings. This may be difficult, but it is necessary to let go of any bottled-up emotions. Friends, family, and even strangers can have an understanding ear. Also seek professional help to share your grief.

My heart is broken; I need your love, period.

I am anxious and afraid; I need you to protect me.

I feel alone; I need you to be with me.

I am misunderstood; I need you to understand me.

I am gasping for breath;
I need you to help me breathe more slowly.

I continue to shed tears; I need you to cry with me.

I am lost in the crowd; I need you to find me.

I cannot process this loss alone;
I need you to be here to share the pain.

—JOAN E.

We have shared our experiences knowing what a gift each and every child is to this world and how sad it is to lose one.

What could you do to soften the grief?

Encourage grieving moms to express their feelings every way they can. Be courageous enough to talk about our precious children. Be there to listen, hug, and share memories so we can find relief, even if only for a moment. We don't need a lot for a short time; we need a little for a long time.

CHAPTER 38

Granting us grace

Such a beautiful word—grace. It represents something we need to give and receive after the loss of a child in various ways.

For us, life is defined either before the tragedy or after. Taking part in a normal conversation is extremely difficult, so we ask for grace when we seem detached.

We cry for no outward reason, yet we simply can't stop the tears. Grant us grace when the tears flow.

Making a decision can be difficult. We doubt ourselves with decision-making because we feel guilty our child died. So we ask for grace when we need to make decisions and struggle doing it.

Being in crowds make us feel more lost and alone than ever, so give us grace if we choose not to go certain places when invited. The things we did before our loss simply aren't as enjoyable as they once were.

Our relationships with others change. Because they are still important, we need a lot of grace here, too. It's strange as well as comforting to be with others who have experienced a loss as deep as ours. We feel immediately safe with them. We teach one another what has helped us and what to expect in the coming weeks, months, and years.

What could you do to soften the grief?

Give us grace by never asking us to stop crying. Our tears are healing, and so is having our safe places. Give us grace, also, as we gravitate to those who will travel with us on this lifelong grief journey.

CHAPTER 39

Our children's memory keepers

Every single day, there's nowhere to stand or turn and not be reminded of our child's being. We converse with our children as if they were here. On occasion, we put ourselves into their shoes and listen. We may hear a "you should have done that a long time ago" or "you shouldn't have done that at all!"

That's why it's a mother's job to keep her child's memory alive and intact.

JANIE *Everyone loves seeing the abundance of butterflies in the warm months. They make us smile as they soothe our souls. When Missy saw a butterfly, she would dance with joy! She was our butterfly—beautiful inside and out.*

The days following Missy's fatal car accident, the butterflies came out in abundance. Everyone noticed. They were landing on family members and hanging out with us as we sat on the patio. Just when I need it most, a sweet butterfly will cross my path. In these Missy moments, my spirits are lifted, and I can continue to move forward.

My friends and family help me in remembering Missy by surprising me with butterfly mementos. I will never tire of these gifts of love—meant for me as well as Missy.

PATTY *Everyone loves Peeps®—those cute, happy sweet treats that come in many shapes, colors, and flavors. Especially my Keeley. When she was a young child, Peeps were only available at Easter as little yellow chicks. Keeley would eat as many Peeps as her parents would allow, and she loved that her brother Hall didn't like Peeps so she'd get his.*

As times have changed, so have Peeps. There are Peeps for Valentine's Day, Easter, July 4th, Halloween, Thanksgiving, and Christmas. They come as chicks, bunnies, hearts, patriot chicks, ghosts, pumpkins, Santa Clauses, or Christmas trees. They even come in flavors of vanilla, chocolate, strawberry, and more.

One recent Easter lunch, my son, daughter-in-law, and grandson brought a beautiful handcrafted basket with grass and Peeps (yellow chicks, of course) for the center-piece. What a delightful surprise! It warmed our hearts to know that Keeley is not only remembered, but that her memory is being shared.

JOAN E *Many times I pull up to the fast-food drive-thru knowing what I want, but out of my mouth comes what my daughter would have ordered. Once when dropping off her sweater at the dry cleaners, I found her Burt's Bees lip balm in the pocket—a small discovery but such a large treasure.*

Surrounded by their photos and mementos, at times we can't bear to look at them for they rip our hearts apart. Other times, we can't look away or get enough of them.

I carry her everywhere with me. Make no mistake, if I'm talking with someone for more than ten minutes, Cindy is there, her face flashing before my eyes or her name sliding across my mind.

It's hard for me to turn loose of anything she wore, touched, or held. These items comfort me as if I'm wrapping myself around her. A mother's memories of her child will never die!

PATTY *You've likely seen the products from company. You've likely seen the products from Life is Good® Company. If you look on the web page* http://content.lifeisgood.com/purpose, *you'll see the following:*

Purpose: Spreading the Power of Optimism.

LIFE IS NOT PERFECT. LIFE IS NOT EASY. LIFE IS GOOD! *My daughter Keeley loved the Life is Good® brand. She had numerous t-shirts, socks, hats, stickers, and whatever else she could find with this logo. Before her cancer diagnosis, she wore this clothing frequently and lived her life with joy. She certainly was aware that life is good, but also hard, challenging, and many times very painful.*

After her cancer diagnosis, it was hard for me to see her wear those Life is Good t-shirts and hats, knowing the difficulty of her journey. After losing her hair from chemotherapy, she had two wigs to wear, but Keeley almost always chose to wear a hat that said Life is Good. A month or so before Keeley's death, she was lying in bed, weak and pale. Of course she was wearing her favorite pink t-shirt with a big daisy and the Life is Good logo. Keeley could see me reading her t-shirt. She said, "Mom, life is good! What a profound statement from a 25-year-old young lady dying from cancer. That's my gal!

As I share memories of Keeley's life with Janie, she often says, "Life is good and so much better because of Keeley."

What could you do to soften the grief?

Even if you never knew our child, make a sincere comment such as "I didn't know your child, but I really feel a closeness to her as well as to you." It will make us feel special.

PART V

GRATEFUL

ACKNOWLEDGMENTS

Acknowledging our children

Dear Missy, Jamie, Keeley, and Cindy,

Thank you for the inspiration you have given us. You took our breath away when you left us. Now, as we begin to breathe again, we are recapturing our lives through this book. For a long time, we could not live in the moment or in the day. We were too busy looking back or worrying forward. Losing you made it hard to restructure our thinking. Today, we are living again.

We also thank you for your role in helping others. As people read *Softening the Grief*, they can now look at the bereaved mothers in their lives and know what to do or say to soften the sad feelings—including the phrase "I have no words."

We love you always.

Your moms

Dear reader,

Please take a few moments to get to know our lost children in the pages that follow.

Janie, Suzie, Patty, Joan

Melissa Dawn Fields

(FEBRUARY 25, 1982-MAY 9, 2004)

Missy was at her best when she was around children. She taught swim lessons as well as being a lifeguard for many summers. She loved kids, and they loved her. She couldn't wait to teach her nephew Garand to swim but unfortunately never got that chance.

Missy had a kind and caring soul. She wanted to work with at-risk kids after college to make a difference in their lives, to help them have a better tomorrow.

Missy's brothers Brian and Kevin and her father and I were certainly blessed when Missy joined our family. She remains a shiny bright spot in our lives.

—JANIE

James (Jamie) Earl Flynt

(MARCH 15, 1972 - FEBRUARY 5, 2007)

 Jamie was my first born and the light of my life. He and I had (I'm really not liking that word "had") a super special bond. We spent a lot of time together taking swim classes, doing arts and crafts, and enjoying gymnastics. I believe boys are always closer to their mommies than girls, and we were "oh so close."

Jamie had an amazing personality with a contagious smile and piercing baby blue eyes—"the window of the soul." No matter the kind of day he was having, we'd still see that smile on his face.

Jamie could always find the positive in any situation that came his way. Ambitious and extremely artistic, he believed everything had to be done correctly or "don't mess with it at all." Affectionate, kind, and joyful, he had the biggest heart of anyone I know.

Jamie was a certified welder specializing in TIG and MIG welding which allowed him to see the world. It was fortunate he was not married and had no children so he could travel wherever he was needed.

I am blessed to have Jamie as my son, though it just wasn't for long enough.

—SUZIE

Keeley Knuteson Hollingsworth

(SEPTEMBER 30, 1983 - JULY 20, 2009)

 Keeley was an energetic, loving, and kind young lady whose life touched many people. She had a giving heart and showed great love for young children, the elderly, the sick, and animals. Her lively free spirit taught many to live life in the moment and to forgive freely.

God regularly blesses us with beautiful stories and signs that reflect Keeley's spirit. We cry often, remember often, and fortunately laugh often when we think about our girl! What a blessing!

—PATTY

"Sometimes you will never know the value of a moment until it becomes a memory."

—DR. SEUSS

Cynthia (Cindy) J. Peterson

(AUGUST 4, 1972 - SEPTEMBER 23, 2013)

"Zip-lining, water rafting, hazing cows were just a few of the things that Mom would do for me. She always had a next adventure or a plan for us. I loved her."

—LUCAS, CINDY'S SON

"I remember the wheatgrass shots and splitting a seaweed salad with her because she was so healthy and wanted us to eat all the right stuff. Being with Mom was always fun. She was so supportive of me and seemed to always be helping others."

—SAMUEL, CINDY'S SON

"I still grin about the Las Vegas trip when I lost all my money at the Golden Nugget. On the cab ride home, my wife told me to put on my seat belt. I said, 'No. I'm feeling lucky tonight.' Cindy laughed all the way home."

—KRIS, CINDY'S BROTHER

"*Raccoons, skunks, cats, dogs, birds, and horses were all the pets so loved by Cindy. But more than her animals, she loved her husband Brent and boys Samuel and Lucas. Her smile and love encompassed too many to mention. Her brother Kris and I were privileged to have loved her as we continue to share stories about our beautiful hell-bent, all-or-nothing, independent gal.*"

What a diverse woman. Daughter, wife, mom, sister, businesswoman, cowgirl. She could transform from president of the Chamber of Commerce to horses and cowboy boots in a flash. She earned a master's degree in Equine Nutrition and Exercise Physiology. Yes, she loved her horses and all variety of animals. When she was in the arena, she gave it her all. Yet, when she walked into a business room she owned it. She had the desire, strength, motivation to take anything on. Except the cancer.

When I lost her, I lost a lot of myself, for she was so much of me. Through this book Softening the Grief, I hope to find myself again in this tribute to my daughter.

—JOAN E.

For Cindy

My need for you continues to grow

For the guidance only you could know

It was always on you I could depend

Even when neither chose to bend

Not realizing when the roles reversed

This mother seeking your insight first

I come still seeking your advice

So as not to pay too heavy a price

Needing you to give me the wisdom

Even for the situations yet to come

My mind so full of heavy turmoil

Sometimes to a simmer others to a boil

Cause there are times can't cope at all

My mind hitting a blank wall

So lean on you still I must

Sometimes the only one to trust

At times I may forget you're gone

Then the hurt and pain hit so strong

Reminding me you are no longer near

Followed by the sudden tear

Looking upward to the sky

I keep asking why why why

—Mom

CINDY

To see you again how I yearn

So please let it be when it is my turn

For I am so certain all these tears

Will never diminish throughout the years

But neither will the vision of your smile

For that was so much your style

And even though your body is gone

Your soul awakens with me every dawn

I always carry it with me

Knowing that is the key

To keeping your memory alive

The only way I can survive

—MOM

Acknowledging ourselves

We bereaved mothers were fortunate to find each other and share our pain. Through writing this book together, we have gained strength while validating our feelings. We hope you have gained as much knowledge and compassion as we have.

Joan E. Markwell

A mother, a grandmother, a wife to husband Denny, I was also Dad's best tomboy. I grew up in Lexington, Kentucky, and became a businesswoman in a variety of venues. I have a love of children, the outdoors, and water. Always ready for the next adventure, I grew up with seven brothers and sisters who, with their families, have been the nucleus of my life. My parents Jo and Bernie Fields just celebrated their 68th wedding anniversary. We have a long, loving family history.

Losing my daughter, Cindy, has taken most of the spunk out of my life. Through *Softening the Grief*, I am slowly regaining my drive by reaching out to others so they may better understand the bereaved mothers in their lives.

Janie Fields

I have been married for 45 years to my high school sweetheart, David, and we've been blessed with three wonderful children. I lost my father 39 years ago and just recently lost my mother. I have one brother who remains a hero in my heart. My two sons are married to wonderful young women, Lisa and Angela, and we have two grandsons, Garand, age 15, and Owen, age four.

I work in technology as an elementary school micro-computer specialist for Fayette County Board of Education in Lexington, Kentucky. I love being with children as they learn new technology! I also love being outdoors, especially working in my many flower gardens. My darling Shih Tzu named Lulu brings much happiness to my heart.

Life without my daughter Missy has changed me in every possible way. I have struggled for so long, but finally after 12 years, I can tell Missy's *life* story instead of her *death* story. She was and will always be my heart and soul.

Patty Hollingsworth

I am a pediatric orthopedic nurse who lost my daughter, Keeley, to cancer in 2009. I have enjoyed a distinguished career, working more than 40 years in this field. For the past 25 years, I've worked at the Shriner's Hospital for Children in Lexington, Kentucky.

When my daughter Keeley was diagnosed with brain cancer at only 23 years of age, I had the formidable task of making the best out of a harrowing situation. Her death left me consumed with grief, anger, fear, loneliness, and depression. After many years of grieving, I've managed to rediscover my faith in life through friendships with others who had also lost a child. They remind me I'm not alone on this hellacious journey and that hope and survival can prevail.

I currently reside in Lexington with my husband of 36 years, Berkeley. We have two beautiful children, Keeley and Hall, a daughter-in-law Crista, and two grandchildren, Winston and Darcy.

Although Keeley ultimately lost her battle to cancer, my love and determination to preserve my daughter's legacy have endured. This book serves as evidence of that. Its words have brought me healing, and I hope it provides the same for others.

Suzie McDonald

Certified in cardiology rehabilitation, I've worked with the same cardiology group in Lexington, Kentucky for the past 30 years. During this time, I've also worked in Cardiac Rehab, Phase II and Phase III, as program director and office manager.

The physicians, nurses, and clergy have always been supportive and understanding after losing my son Jamie.

Jamie was a loving, kind-hearted, handsome young man who was taken from his family and friends far too soon. He made his living as a licensed specialty welder traveling around the world doing what he loved.

Jamie has a younger brother, Chase, he loved and cherished dearly. Since the loss of Jamie, his brother has blessed my husband, Greg, and myself with two beautiful granddaughters and another on the way.

I always called Jamie "free spirited" and now I refer to him as my Free-Spirited Angel. Our family was blessed to have had Jamie as long as we did. He will always be loved and remembered.

A final word
from the authors

If you felt it was a gift to know our child, then we ask you to continue to share that gift. Remember that we hurt every day. Your gifts of remembrance validate our feelings that our child was and continues to be loved, missed, and never forgotten. You can help to keep us strong so we are able to stand and reach out to the next unfortunate mother who experiences the pain of losing a child. It's never too late and the relationship was never too long ago to mention our child.

Made in the USA
Lexington, KY
07 August 2017